BA

P9-DEV-323

THE CUB FAN'S GUIDE TO LIFE

THE CUB FAN'S GUIDE TO LIFE

The Ultimate Self-Help Book

Jim Langford

Diamond Communications, Inc.
PO Box 94
Notre Dame, IN 46556

1984

THE CUB FAN'S GUIDE TO LIFE
Copyright © 1984 by Diamond Communications, Inc.

Diamond books are available at special quantity discounts for bulk purchases for sales premiums, sales promotions, premiums, fundraising, or educational use. For details, write to:
Diamond Communications, Inc.
PO Box 94
Notre Dame, IN 46556
Or call: (219) 287-5008

Library of Congress Cataloging in Publication Data

Langford, Jim.

The cub fan's guide to life.

1. Baseball—Fans—Anecdotes, facetiae, satire, etc. 2. Chicago Cubs (Baseball team)—Anecdotes, facetiae, satire, etc. I. Title.
PN6231.B35L3 1984   818'.5402   84-12695
ISBN 0—912083-08-5 (pbk.)

Manufactured in the United States of America

This book is dedicated
with love
to
Jill Ann Justice Langford
my wife
my best friend
and
my publisher

CONTENTS

FOREWORD

FOREWORD

A Cub fan friend of mine put it well recently. (Now that's redundant—how can he be a friend without being a Cub fan?) He said, "If my colonel told me we had to take that pillbox no matter what the cost in life and limb, I'd ask to take five Cub fans with me—because from the day they're born, Cub fans know danger, pain, suffering, etc."

He's right. What creature on earth has battled the odds longer than the Cub fan and his descendants? Who else has waited since 1908 for a World Series winner? Yes—1908—when Teddy Roosevelt was president and there were only 45 states in the Union.

Yet there he is—almost every day—sitting in the bleachers holding hands with his Cub fan girl friend—enjoying the box seat his family has had for years—chatting with his senior citizen neighbors and second-guessing one move after another in, as Ernie Banks put it, "God's own sunshine."

Dinner's going to be late. So what? What are we supposed to do—leave before it's over just because it's in extra innings?

Rent's a little overdue—so's the bank loan. Hadn't thought about that since the first inning. Let's talk about important things. Just as sure as you're born the Cardinal pitcher balked on that pickoff and not one of the umpires caught itñ Oh, well— we've got the top of the batting order up next inning . . .

That's the stuff Cub fans are made of. Jim Langford's book exemplifies the devotion and humor that go with being a Cub fan. Here's hoping you enjoy it.

Jack Brickhouse

1. INTRODUCTION

INTRODUCTION

Most self-help books today play the march of the age. They aim to make you more assertive, aggressive, strident and competitive than you ever dreamed you could be. If you follow the lead of the "me-first" self-help guides, you may make it to the top of your profession but the steps of the ladder will be the broken spirits of the colleagues, loved ones, and strangers you have trampled along the way. Follow the precepts of this enlightened selfishness and you'll end up so crooked they'll have to screw you into the ground when you die.

Be honest. Haven't you bought in to the "Be all you can be" philosophy? Do you seethe everytime some driver cuts in front of you, not because it costs you a few seconds but because someone has beaten you out? Do you find that your ego, your whole self is on the line every time you have an argument even over trivial matters such as who is going to take the garbage out? Do you worry about what others say about you behind your back? Do you think that a cool reaction to a put-down makes you mousey? If so, this book is for you.

On the other hand, do you feel like a nameless, faceless speck in the universe: alone, alienated, without affiliation and fraternity? Are you so hard up for community that you think you're part of a special breed because you have a Gold Visa Card? Have you ever felt like stopping in the middle of the herd rushing to the El train, stomping your foot and yelling, "I AM A PERSON!"? If so, this book is for you.

In the pages that follow, I am going to show you that there is more to life than winning. Happiness doesn't necessarily come with a promotion, a conquest, or a league championship. I will show you how to be a winner in the real sense of the word.

Once you open your mind to the miracle of Cub fan therapy, the $3.95 you spent on this book may turn out to be the best investment you've ever made. But just as there are no guarantees in life, there aren't any on this book either. So don't ask for your money back.

2. TESTING YOUR CUB FAN QUOTIENT

TESTING YOUR CUB FAN QUOTIENT

How are you going to know whether or not Cub fan therapy can help you unless you measure where you're coming from? Here is a simple attitude inventory designed to give you a pretty good picture of how you see yourself and life in general right now. Mark your answers quickly and decisively and don't go back and change them. If you cheat, you owe me a $5.00 fine (cash only, please).

1. Pick the statement that most accurately expresses your belief:
_____"Nice guys finish last."
_____"Winning isn't everything, it's the only thing."
_____"You have to be prepared for adversity."
_____"Only rats desert a sinking ship."

2. The Cubs are losing 5-0 with two outs in the 9th. You decide to:
_____get to your car and beat the traffic.
_____position yourself near the Cub dugout so you can insult the losers.
_____vow not to come back until the Cubs improve.
_____hope for a game-winning rally.

3. Your best friend has caused you heartache for thirty-eight years. You resolve:

_____ you've stood by long enough; it's
time to give up.

_____ to focus on the thrills and good
times.

_____ to protect yourself from further hurt
by moderating your affection.

_____ to stand by your friend as long as
you live.

4. Suppose the Cubs finish last. Your reaction would be:

_____ switch allegiance to the White Sox
or Cardinals.

_____ it doesn't matter; you expected it.

_____ point out that this was the best team
ever to finish last.

_____ buy season tickets for next year.

5. Suppose you could have one wish
granted. You would choose:

_____ to marry a movie star.

_____ to pitch the Cubs to a pennant.

_____ five million dollars in cash.

_____ to live long enough to see the Cubs
win a World Series.

6. You are locked in a barn with a ton of
horse manure. You respond by:

_____ cursing your fate.

_____ searching for a pony.

_____complaining about the stench.
_____thinking about what great fertilizer
       you'll have when you get out.

7. The Cubs win six in a row. Your response
is to:

_____feel that this is too good to last and
       that they'll lose today.
_____start thinking pennant.
_____enjoy it, bask in it, but take it in
       stride.
_____wear the same clothes every day un-
       til they lose.

8. The Cubs have lost five in a row. You're
thinking:

_____the odds are with us to win.
_____it's still a long way to our record of
       13 losses in a row.
_____now we'll start an 8-game winning
       streak.
_____this is typical.

9. The Cubs win only 7 of 28 games in
spring training. You're thinking:

_____spring training doesn't matter.
_____our rookies look great and we will
       be contenders.
_____this is typical.

10. Attendance isn't enough to pay great players. You think that:

_____we need lights at Wrigley Field.

_____we should build a new park.

_____we should sell more beer signs.

_____we need winning baseball, not night baseball.

ANSWERS TO THE
CUB FAN QUOTIENT TEST

answer	point value	comments
1. "Nice guys finish last."	1	Only sometimes.
"Winning isn't everything, it's the only thing."	0	You must be fun to live with!
"You have to be prepared for adversity."	9	You can still do that and be an optimist.
"Only rats desert a sinking ship."	9	Remember that those who stay with it and salvage it, get the treasure.

2. "get to your car and beat the traffic." — 0 — You obviously don't believe in rallies.

   "position yourself near the Cub dugout so you can insult the losers." — -2 — Shame on you!

   "vow not to come back until the Cubs improve." — 3 — See you tomorrow!

   "hope for a game-winning rally." — 10 — That's the spirit!

3. "you've stood by long enough; it's time to give up." — 1 — You get a point for your 38 years, but that's all.

   "to focus on the thrills and good times." — 9 — You can't beat fun at the old ballpark, can you?

   "to protect yourself from further hurt by moderating your affection." — 5 — That's an understandable, if chicken-hearted reaction.

   "to stand by your friend as long as you live." — 10 — This Bud's for you!

4. "switch allegiance to the White Sox or Cardinals." — -4 — We got along without 'ya before we met 'ya; we'll get along without 'ya now.

11

"it doesn't matter; you expected it."	3	Even if you expected it, it *does* matter.
"point out that this is the best team ever to finish last."	8	Consider, for example, the 1966 Cubs.
"buy season tickets for next year."	10	That's putting your money where your heart is!

5. "to marry a movie star." — 5 — After all, you're only human.

"to pitch the Cubs to a pennant." — 10 — We can use you.

"five million dollars in cash." — 0 — You can't buy happiness.

"to live long enough to see the Cubs win the World Series." — 8 — Don't you already plan to live another year or two?

6. "cursing your fate." — 0 — Don't be such a wimp!

"searching for a pony." — 10 — Even in the bad years we had Ernie Banks.

"complaining about the stench." — 0 — Whining isn't always cured by winning.

"thinking about what great fertilizer you'll have when you get out." — 9 — You've definitely got character!

7. "feel that this is too good to last and that they'll lose today." — 2 — Two points for honesty.

"start thinking pennant." — 8 — A real Cub fan starts thinking pennant after 3 wins in a row.

"enjoy it, bask in it, but take it in stride." — 8 — How can you be cool after six straight wins?

"wear the same clothes everyday until they lose." — 9 — You'll find out if your relatives really love you.

8. "the odds are with us to win." — 8 — You should know better than to count on the odds.

"it's still a long way to our record of 13 losses in a row." — 6 — That's true, but it's negative thinking.

"now we'll start an 8-game winning streak." — 9 — Why only 8?

"this is typical." — 2 — Work on your attitude!

13

9. "spring training doesn't matter." — 7 — Spring matters but the exhibition games don't.

"our rookies look great and we'll be contenders." — 10 — That's the ticket!

"this is typical." — 0 — Work on your attitude.

10. "we need lights at Wrigley Field." — 0 — Or, we could play in the dark.

"we should build a new stadium." — 5 — And still use Wrigley Field for day games.

"We should sell more beer signs." — 5 — If selling beer signs pays for Lee Smith, sell more!

"We need winning baseball, not night baseball." — 10 — Ain't that the truth!

Now check the answers and score yourself accordingly. Your total points are _____. Where does this place you on the following scale?

    0-35 . . . You should be a Yankee fan!
  36-60 . . . You need this book!
  61-90 . . . Your instincts are good; develop them!
  91-98 . . . You're already a great person!

(I made it impossible to score 100 on the test just to remind you that nobody's perfect, as every Cub fan knows.)

3. CUB FAN THERAPY

CUB FAN THERAPY

It's tough to be happy. We're led to think that happiness is something instant; just add water and you've got it made. Snort a little coke and you'll feel great. Make a short-lived conquest and you'll feel worthwhile. Adopt the latest style, cheer for the team that's winning this year and you can be part of the crowd.

It doesn't take long to find out that real happiness can't be freeze-dried. Being part of the crowd loses some of its allurement when we discover that it's a lonely crowd. The trouble with most of us is that we are selling ourselves short. In our frenzy to cater to what others want or expect of us, we let *their* tastes dictate our desires.

There is only one real way out of the contemporary trap and that is to get our egos in shape by developing those habits that used to be called virtues. The key to enduring happiness is a strong inner-self, a self built on character, formed by hard work and kept strong by the daily practice of the virtues. That is the program that we call Cub Fan Therapy.

To be a true Cub fan is to see somebody worthwhile in the mirror. Cub Fan Therapy offers a philosophy of life that can deal with good and evil, pain and pleasure, apparent failure and passing success—and even heartbreak. The Greek philosopher Aristotle wrote in 340 B.C. that virtue is necessary for happiness and that three things are required for virtue: first, knowledge; second, to choose wisely; and third, to act in a firm and steadfast manner. He didn't know it, of course, but he was describing the Cub fan. To be a Cub fan is to be a graduate student in the school of life. What can life possibly offer or throw at us that we haven't known before?

We've known glory. Those *ignorami* who ridicule Cub fans for staying with a loser have no sense of history. The Cubs are not one year. Or ten. Or fifty. There have been Cubs since 1876 and they have won sixteen league championships, ten of them since 1900. No professional sports team has won as many games as the Cubs have. No major league team has ever equalled the one hundred and sixteen victories in one season notched by the 1906 Cubs. No wonder the Law of Averages has given other teams the last thirty-eight years to catch up with us!

We've known pain, suffering and deprivation. For Cub fans the National League became a desert in 1946. But show me a people who haven't had to work their way through a desert or conquer a wilderness and I'll show you a colony of wimps. Happiness always lies on the other side of tribulations and only those with staying power will attain it.

We've known disappointment. If you don't expect much, you'll never know real disappointment. In 1969 and 1970, Cub fans expected a pennant. On paper we had the best team in baseball. In 1969 we held first place from opening day until September 10. And we lost. To the Mets! We had to listen to everything from the gloating of White Sox fans to the opinion of a psychiatrist who explained that the Cubs folded because they were afraid of heights. To say that our spirits were tested would be putting it mildly. Yet we stuck with our Cubs and cheered on knowing that it was the last hurrah of a team we had watched grow for seven years and that its like would not come our way again for another fifteen years or more. Does that tell you something about loyalty and forgiveness and even that it's O.K. to cry?

And through it all, *we've known pleasure:* the pleasure of game-winning home runs by Hank Sauer, the meteoric rise of Dick Drott or Bob Speake, the joy of having Ernie Banks play his whole career for us, the heroics of no-hitters by Sam Jones, Don Cardwell, Burt Hooton, Milt Pappas; the gracefulness of Santo, Kessinger, Sandberg, and Jenkins; the perfect swing of Billy Williams. The list could go on and on.

The point is that you cannot be a Cub fan for long without beginning to grow from day to day in those virtues that lead to happiness. Let me illustrate what I mean:

FAITH

Do you remember that blasted Tug McGraw jumping up in the air and yelling, "You gotta believe" as he helped the Mets to the pennant in 1969? (I remember too and I will be glad when he and Seaver, Ryan, Koosman and Staub finally retire and the last vestiges of that bunch can no longer harm us in uniform.) The truth is that McGraw's plea for faith was nothing more than plagiarism. I'll tell you about belief! Faith is what enables you to go beyond the evidence and reach the intangible. Cub fans were believing before McGraw was born. Don't misunderstand. Cub fans are not naive. We didn't believe all the hype and promises made by the front office that the Cubs would win the pennant in 1950, 51,52,53, . . . etc. You didn't see us lining up for World Series tickets in January when general manager Wid Matthews told us we'd win the pennant if Bruce Edwards' arm stopped being sore. Our belief is more fundamental than that. What we believe is that someday—maybe this year—the Cubs will win it all. When the time is right, it will happen. Fate will find a way.

HOPE

Psychiatrists tell us that two essential ingredients in mental health and personal happiness are self esteem and the virtue of hope. Cub fans have the patent on hope. If it didn't exist, we would have invented it. Even knowing that Ken Kravec was starting against Steve Carlton, a real Cub fan would turn on the radio to find out if we won.

Ancient pagan rituals were built around Spring as the harbinger of new life and new hope for the tribe. In Spring our tribe too thinks of revival and we listen intently to reports coming up from Mesa, Arizona. Does it matter that the official hosts of the Cubs in spring training are a group called the Ho-Ho Kams, named after an Indian tribe that mysteriously disappeared? No, what matters is that we begin to hear how newly-acquired veterans and stellar rookie prospects will give the Cubs a new look, a new chance this year. We're looking for words like "dazzling catch," "blinding speed," "major-league curve," and "power to burn." Sure, we like spring phenoms. But most of all, we like to hope.

It is our hope that inspires our optimism. We look at the bright side. Listen to Bert Wilson; "The Cubs are trailing nine to one, there are two outs and nobody on in the bottom of the ninth. Here's Preston Ward, hitting .206. Remember, fans, the game is never over until the last man is out. C'mon, Pres, hit one."

Listen to sportswriter Steve Daley: "A Cub fan sees diamonds where others see broken glass. Give the man or woman in the bleachers the genuine article—a Banks, a Williams, a Buckner—and they'll follow you anywhere."

Listen to Hall-of-Fame announcer Jack Brickhouse: "So the Cubs have not won a pennant in nearly forty years. Look at it this way: in terms of eternity that's not even a flyspeck. Just tell yourself that some time in the next one thousand years the Cubs will get their share of the pie."

CHARITY

Cub fans know a lot about love. Even if our team has been something like a wayward spouse, we have the kind of strength that enables us to go on accepting our favorites, flaws and all.

Cub fans have never wanted to rival Philly fans as boo birds. But just because we are not rude does not mean that we are uncritical. It is simply that we are willing to applaud an all-out effort more than we are to punish for imperfection. Our love is devoted but not submissive, sensitive but not weak, trusting but not gullible, tolerant but not indifferent, tender but not sentimental.

Almost everyone who has worn the Cub uniform has a claim on our affection. We cherish the brief but shining moments of Frank Ernaga, Cuno Barragan, Ellis Burton, Steve Dillard and Jim Qualls as well as the decades of excellence provided by Ernie, Billy, Ron, Glenn, Fergie, Philibuck, and Jolly Cholly.

The point is that our love is not fair-weather, not reserved only for the greatest. Above all, it is a love that knows how to accept, how to forgive, how to trust, how to persevere. There is no such thing as an ex-Cub fan!

PATIENCE

Fans of long standing know that the last time the Cubs won a World Championship was in 1908. We have won pennants six times since then but each time we lost the World Series. And how many "five-year plans" have we endured since 1945? We put up with Wid Matthews telling us one year that the Cubs were launching a youth movement and playing guys that would have had trouble in Des Moines. Then the next year Wid would promise to season the team with experienced veterans. Remember how we had Ralph Kiner, Howie Pollet, Walker Cooper, Monte Irvin, Al Dark, Richie Ashburn, Robin Roberts, etc. long after their prime?

We lived through the college of coaches in the early sixties, the trade of Lou Brock, the crash of '69, the giving away of Bill Madlock and through it all, only once did the fans storm the executive offices at Wrigley Field.

Remember the next time you're in a traffic jam or waiting to get your driver's license renewed, or standing in line at the post office, you're a Cub fan; you can handle the wait. While others around you are cursing, making obscene gestures and generally losing it, you, the Cub fan, can maintain your inner cool. You've waited a long, long time for something more important than mailing a package; you've been waiting for a pennant.

PERSEVERANCE

Perseverance is having the grit to hold your allegiance in place no matter what. Set the test and see if a Cub fan can endure it. Roy Smalley's errant throws to first? A piece of cake. Dave Kingman's adventures with fly balls? We seldom even booed. Herman Franks as General Manager? The collapse of 1969? A *tenth* place finish in 1966? We're still here. We still care. Our legendary adherence comes from yet another virtue, namely:

FORTITUDE

Cub fans aren't afraid of hardship. We don't waver in the face of bombast; we love to confound gloating White Sox fans who think that they can rile us by mocking, scoffing at and insulting our Cubs. We aren't deterred by the problem of parking near Wrigley Field. We didn't even stay away when we knew that we'd be watching Roberto Peña play shortstop. It is our courage that leads to our

TEMPERANCE

Do you want evidence of our self-control? You don't see Cub fans pouring cups of beer from the upper deck onto the patrons below. Cardinal fans who can't take losing do stuff like that. Unlike another park in Chicago, Wrigley Field has never had its sod torn up by rampaging rioters, never had a disco demolition, never needed to hire bodyguards to protect the patrons from each other. Na-Na-Na-Na, Hey - Hey, Goodbye. Moderation in all things.

KNOWLEDGE

A major ingredient in the formula for a successful life is knowledge. It is important to know as much about as many things as is humanly possible. Here again, Cub fans excel. The left field bleachers alone could supply enough managers to stock the major leagues many times over. And if you picked a random sample of fans from every ballpark in the country and had a baseball quiz bowl, the Wrigleyfielders would win going away. If you don't believe that, ask your grandmother to show you how Dee Fondy held the bat when he was going to lay down a drag bunt. For Cub fans, knowledge over time grows into

WISDOM

At first glance it may not seem that a truly wise person would be a Cub fan. Ah but have you ever noticed the wry smile on a Cub fan's face as some bore attacks the Cubs at a cocktail party? It is a smile that comes from the acceptance of reality, from an inner peace, and from the certainty that before long the Cubs will win it all. Just as the world is round, history is cyclical; it repeats itself. The pennant in 1945 was not the pennant to end all pennants. No one thought that in 1935 the Cubs would win their last twenty-two games in a row and take the flag. But they did. Not even the Yankees have been perpetually strong. Not even the Mets have been perpetually weak. With wisdom as an ally, the Cub fan waits. And smiles knowingly.

Having reviewed the various virtues that constitute Cub fan therapy, it's time to tell a couple of true stories that show how they apply in real life.

1. THE PERSONALITY KID

Way back in the late 1940's when the Cubs were lucky to finish eighth in an eight-team league, it was an annual custom to hear brave predictions from Cub managers that the pennant was only a season away. Alas, most often the rookies failed and the veterans faded, leaving the Cubs at home in the basement by June 6th. Fans wanted to know why. Sportswriters were merciless in their mockery. And owner Philip K. Wrigley went public with his own bafflement over the causes of continued mediocrity.

In 1950, Mr. Wrigley began receiving letters, telegrams and phone calls from someone in St. Paul, Minnesota. The message was simple: what the Cubs need is a manager who could instill a winning spirit. The author of the messages offered to take the job and he signed himself "The Personality Kid."

As far as I can tell, Mr. Wrigley never hired "The Personality Kid" (unless at a much later date and it was Leo Durocher or Herman Franks). But for all I know, he was tempted. He had tried everything else and a decade later he hired a college of coaches and an athletic director.

* * * * * *

In 1983, a rabid Cub fan, transplanted from Chicago to Springerville, Arizona, heard that there was an opening in the front office of the Iowa Cubs, the AAA affiliate of the Chicago Cubs in Des Moines, Iowa. His name: Bill Holden. He had met his bride-to-be for the first time at the Cubs exhibition game in Scottsdale. They were both teachers, both Cub fans, and they fell in love, married and began their family.

Now Bill Holden did what most red-blooded Cub fans only dream of doing. He decided to get that job with the Iowa Cubs. With his wife's blessing, he quit his job as a high school teacher and baseball coach, packed up his family and moved from Arizona to Des Moines. He went to Sec Taylor Stadium and filled out an application, wrote numerous letters to the club officials outlining his ideas, and called club president Ken Grandquist until he was given an interview. Bill Holden did "The Personality Kid" one better; he got the job! Hats off to the owners who hired him. Hats off to the wife who shared his fantasy. Hats off to Bill Holden. The Personality Kid lives and he's a Cub!

2. MY OWN STORY

Whatever happens in your life, Cub fan therapy can teach you the miracle of acceptance. Some years ago, I experienced a series of setbacks and lost almost everything I had. For a while I lived in a cheap, efficiency apartment, then in a friend's basement. Finally I was able to move into a new apartment and I was thrilled to start furnishing it. After a year there it was beginning to look great; more than that, I had a place I could call *home.* Then came a violent spring storm. A huge maple tree crashed through the roof of one of the apartment buildings in my complex. It was the building I lived in. In fact, it came to rest in my living room. All of my things were soaked with rain and gummy insulation.

As I made my way through the gawkers who seem to gather wherever there is disaster, I was met by the owner of the complex. He asked whether I had tenant's insurance. I said "No." He said how sorry he was for me. Then, from strength built up over years of June swoons and late inning losses (in other words from my life as a Cub fan), I summoned the words that proved to me once and for all that I could withstand anything; that, like the Cubs, I could go on rebuilding for as long as it took. I said, "It's O.K., I'm a Cub fan. I've seen worse crashes than this." I've learned that material things really don't matter. What's important is the willingness to get up and go on. Cub fans do that every year!

4. DESIDERIUM

It's time for a little inspiration. Put the 1812
Overture on your stereo and read this aloud:

DESIDERIUM

Though the shakey violets around you
may wither,
plant your Cub flag
and stand firm;
No swoon, no storm can rob you of
your hope.

Even if you hear that your heroes
scored fourteen runs and still
lost by two, stand by them.
No one promised you a rose garden;
settle for ivy-covered bricks.

If those you love renounce you
remember how Roy Smalley changed
boos to cheers
with one swing of the bat.
Aim for the fences
even if you do
strike out a lot.
Always throw your fastball,
but also learn
to duck.

THE CUB FAN'S GUIDE TO LIFE

Forty years of waiting
is but a speck in
the cosmic flow of time;
a few more won't matter.
Remember, when all looks hopeless,
the game is never over
until the last man is out.

For a good time,
call 281-5050
and ask for
box seats.

When you see ex-Cubs on
pennant-winning teams,
remind yourself that
they had their chance with us
and muffed it.

Take solace in the knowledge
that, whatever else can be said of you,
you didn't trade Brock for Broglio.

If you think that Fate
has it in for your favorites,
think of the Bulls, the Bears,
and Northwestern football.

Desiderium

Be not troubled by falls or failures,
by slowness or a high ERA.
You know that every losing streak
must end,
and when it does, a winning streak
of one has already begun.

It is better to have swung
and missed
than never to have swung
at all.

Give thanks to your Creator
for all that made you what you are.
And if you don't think that's much,
ponder this:
You could have been a Mets fan.
Or a Sox fan.
Or a Cardinals fan.

Know that even if it seems
that your wheels have spun
for years and gotten you nowhere,
you can handle it!
A lesser being might yield to despair.
But not you.
You've been there.

You're a Cub fan!
You're the best!

5. A MYTH FOR CUB FANKIND

A MYTH FOR CUB FANKIND

Every great civilization or movement has its own special myth, its own symbolic story that tells of its goals, trials, virtues, and ultimate victory. There is even a myth for Cub fankind. The Myth of Sisyphus dates back to ancient Greece but it was adapted by the French philosopher Albert Camus, who used it to symbolize the fate of the human condition. If it seems a bit pessimistic, it is because Camus was writing during the devastation of World War II. The story goes like this:

Sisyphus, condemned for stealing the secrets of the gods, was sentenced to a terrible punishment. He was made to spend time and eternity rolling a boulder to the top of a mountain. Every time he reached the top the boulder would fall back to the bottom and it was his duty to go down and start over. It was to be a forever of futile and hopeless labor.

But myths are made for the imagination to breathe life into them. There is Sisyphus working, pushing, trying; he gets higher and higher. And then the

41

boulder slips. It is at that point that the fainthearted and fair-weather fan gives up. It is at that point that we come not to pity or laugh at Sisyphus but to *admire* him. Why? Because he goes back down to the foot of the mountain knowing it is a torment that will never end. But in doing so, he is superior to his fate; he is harder and stronger than that boulder, taller than that mountain. The gods thought he would suffer because he knew how helpless he was before he even started. What they didn't reckon on is that there is no fate that cannot be overcome by acceptance. Sisyphus becomes the master of his fate. Even if he never gets the boulder to the top to stay (past September 10th), every time he goes down and begins again he confirms the higher faithfulness that negates the punishment. The struggle itself toward the heights is enough to fill a man's heart. It is enough to make him happy.

For long-time Cub fans, the Myth of Sisyphus paints a dramatic picture of the Cub condition. They remember how, year after year, from 1948 on, the Cubs would surge in May, climb to the top and rest there just long enough for the repetition of a classic June Swoon. Back to the bottom by the fourth of July.

But one can take a longer view and see the myth as it portrays the whole decade of the 1960s. It opened with the college of coaches, those revolving mentors who roamed the country erasing the distinction between major league and minor league Cubs by preaching and teaching the same message to all.

For the first half of the decade, the Cubs seldom rose high enough even to swoon. Leo Durocher came in proclaiming that this was not an eighth place ball club and proved himself correct by proceeding to finish tenth in an expanded league. But then the talent that had come up through the farm system (perhaps even aided by the college of coaches!) began to assert itself. Santo, Williams, Holtzman, Nye, Niekro, and Kessinger joined Banks, Hundley, Jenkins, Hands and Hickman and the push was on. In 1969, they raised the boulder to the top and actually rested there for one hundred and fifty-five days before the crushing fall from laureate to laughing stock. Again, in 1970, they rose to the summit. But like sand in an hour glass, once more they slipped quietly, inexorably from the top. With only short-lived exceptions, the Cubs have spent the last decade near the bottom of the mountain. Able only on occasion to launch an assault on the heights, they have taught their fans that even though every chapter in the saga may end up being a new frustration, it is also and always a new beginning.

And now, in 1984, our Don Quijotes of the diamond are ready once again to carry their burden to the top. Cub fans cheer the quest; the struggle itself is enough to endure if not overcome the thirty-eight-year-old curse. It is impossible to break hope if it chooses not to be broken. Cub fans live by hope in the face of fate. It is our reason to go on, to take the next step. We will never believe that our goal is unattainable. Not all of the magic doors have been tried yet.

For the first time in fourteen years the Cubs have power, speed, defense and spirit all on the same team and at the same time. There is nothing in the idea of hope that stops us from knowing that we could use a little more pitching. But baseball is a game not only of skill, but also of chance and circumstance. The 1969 Cubs were one of the most talented teams in recent baseball history. But fate (and platooning) favored the Mets. Look who is platooning this year; Yes! The Cubs! Fate cannot be far behind. The great flood in the Book of Genesis lasted for only forty days and forty nights. The Thirty Years War in Europe lasted for only thirty years. The end of our exile in the desert is near. But what if it doesn't happen this year?

A Myth for Cub Fankind

The real Cub fan refuses the blindfold and smiles at the would-be executioner. The way to defeat fate is to face it. If we have to push the rock up the mountain again and again, we will do it knowingly and without flinching. Why? Because one year, maybe this year—or next—the powers who condemned us like Sisyphus will realize that we are stronger than their punishment. Their admiration for our true grit will compel them to restore the law of averages. Then the wind will blow for us and against Mike Schmitt. Then opposing fielders will drop flyballs, misplay grounders and miss the cutoff man. Then pebbles in the infield will deflect our routine outs and make them into doubles. All of the games we have given away will be given back to us. That is what transforms a good team into a team of destiny. And it's our turn!

And on the day the Cubs clinch the championship, Wrigley Field will be jammed with fans. Their collective hope will simply carry the winning home run (like Gabby Hartnett's in 1938) all the way to the bleachers. I, for one, hope that it is hit off of Tug McGraw. On that day we will rest on top of the mountain. The stone will stay on top of the mountain as a monument to that hope that is stronger than fate itself. It is inevitable! It will happen soon! The Cubs will be champions!

6. ON RAISING CHILDREN

ON RAISING CHILDREN

There are hundreds of books on the market which are designed to answer that age-old question, "How can I do a good job raising my children?" The problem goes all the way back to Adam and Eve. Of their first two kids, one turned out to be a murderer and the other a victim. Too bad they didn't have a copy of Dr. Spock or *Parent Effectiveness Training* to read.

If you're a Cub fan, you don't need a myriad of psychologically-loaded theories telling you how to be a good parent. All you have to do is review your Cub history and build your own system by adapting the styles of various Cub managers from the past. If your little Cubs are too docile, sloppy, lazy, unmotivated, or selfish, cocky and brash, you need only imagine yourself as a manager in pinstripes with a big C on your chest and to choose the right style needed to promote each stage of your child's development.

Let's review the styles you can choose from:

Rogers Hornsby: be aggressive, sharp-tongued and settle for nothing less than perfection. Seek to be feared more than loved.

Charlie Grimm: be knowledgeable; be patient; use your sense of humor to keep them loose. Inspire them to want to do well because of their real affection for you.

Frankie Frisch: Try innovative ways to teach them good habits. If your pitchers can't find the plate, give your catcher a white mitt to make a better target. Get the idea? Put up posters with inspirational messages like "Winning is a Habit—Catch the Habit!" Or "For a Good Time, Be a Winner for a Change!" Insist on head-first slides as a sign of spirit.

Stan Hack: Always be gentle and kind. Smile your way through every crisis. Be their friend through thin and thin.

Leo Durocher: Work them until their little tongues hang out. When things are going well, bolt for a couple of days without telling anyone where you are. Build their confidence by bragging about them in public. But when you're mad at them, let them have it in front of their siblings and friends. Above all, keep them off guard!

Jim Marshall: Give them lots of leeway in the hope that they will mature. Then blame yourself when they don't.

Preston Gomez: Wonder aloud why you ever decided to have kids in the first place.

Herman Franks: Spit a lot. If you've got a star in the bullpen, use him until his arm falls off. Always apply strategy. Make sure your left-handed kids get right-handed teachers. If things don't work out, single out the prima donnas, blast them, and resign.

Lee Elia: Defend your kids at all costs. If someone picks on them give the *!##*'s a chewing out they'll never forget. Keep your fingers crossed that your loyalty to your kids will evoke some performance in return.

Jim Frey: Bring out the best in each kid. Be honest but also diplomatic. Be positive but also realistic. Lead with quiet determination. Explain why, if there's only one deck of cards, they can't all play solitaire at the same time.

Now obviously, no one style of management is perfect for all stages of a cub's development. The secret is to use the right tactic for each stage. Here are my recommendations:

For age 1-2: Use the Stan Hack approach of unconditional affirmation. Always be warm and nice. Coax but don't cajole.

For age 3-6: Use the Frankie Frisch method. Be creative; inspire; try to teach the fundamentals. Put up a poster of the Old Cub Fan "Waiting for a Pennant." (Available from Diamond Communications)

For age 7-10: Adopt the Marshall Plan. Give them some rope; let them know what you expect. Let them see you suffer a little bit when they fail.

For age 11: Employ the Elia defense mechanism. Your kids will know that you'll stand by them all the way to the wall.

For age 12-13: Be like Leo Durocher. Put them in the lineup and keep them there; tell them they can rest when you're ready to let them rest.

Never use the bench. Accept no sub-stitutions. Build their confidence by bragging about them, for example, "My kid is worth three Gary Cole-mans." But be ready to blast them when they have a sub-par day. Above all, don't let them figure you out or take you for granted.

For age 14-15: Time to make them reach. Use the Hornsby rule. You're going to be natural enemies anyway, so set perfection as the only accep-table norm and let them know who their judge is.

For age 16: When you're overwhelmed by loud music, strange behavior, and demands for money; when you find the medicine cabinet filled with pimple remedies and hair dressings, let them hear you echo the famous words of Preston Gomez: "If I had known then what I know now, I never would have taken this job."

For age 17-18: They're ready now for the Herman Franks treatment. Re-gard them as cogs in your machine. Establish a pattern and stick to it. If they don't do it your way, surprise them: instead of kicking *them* out, just quit and go make a million bucks in real estate.

For age 19-20: They are ready now for Charlie Grimm's kind of leadership. Be yourself with them; lead by example. Let your kindness, your humor and your knowledge of the game of life be their inspiration. They will love you and be proud to please you. Now they're ready for life's pennant race.

For age 21: Adopt the Jim Frey method. Show them how to put all the pieces together and go for it!

These are, of course, just one fan's recommendations. You may wish to make adjustments according to your own experience of Cub history or in light of the material you have to work with. Naturally, some cautions need to be exercized in applying your managerial approach to child rearing. Please remember to discourage stealing and hitting in favor of control and sacrifice.

It probably should be mentioned, too, that there are extreme options you may have to consider along the way:

Trade—use only in extreme circumstances.

Unconditional release—if they are still home at age 25, this is a real possibility.

Fines—you might get away with this if they don't have agents yet.

The College of Coaches approach—If they are really causing you problems, get relatives, in-laws, etc. to take turns managing them. This will keep them confused right up to their 21st birthday. Then you can put them on waivers.

Good luck and good managing! Remember, the sanity you save may be your own!

7. LETTERS TO DR. DIE-HARD

LETTERS TO DR. DIE-HARD

Dear Dr. Die-Hard:

Help! My mother-in-law is coming to stay with us for three weeks. She drinks so much beer that I'm thinking about renting an extra refrigerator so we can keep some food in ours. I don't know what I am going to do with her; all she ever does is make a mess, pick fights, and spout obscenities.

Signed,

Perplexed in Berywn

Dear P.I.B.:

Show her how to catch the El train to Comiskey Park.

D.H.

Dear Dr. Die-Hard:

I'm 45 years old and I keep having the same dream night after night. In it, I win a contest and get to pitch batting practice at Wrigley Field. My knuckleball baffles the hitters, the Cubs sign me up and my relief pitching leads them to the pennant. How do you interpret this?

Signed,

Dreamy Dwight

Dear D.D.:

I've had almost the same dream. But I've got a better chance than you do because the Cubs already have a great bullpen. I'm going to be a starter.

D.H.

Dear Dr. Die-Hard:

What do you think of the saying that "Nice guys finish last?"

Signed,

Fannie Zuckerman

Dear Fannie:

I've never believed it. Charlie Grimm was a nice guy and he helped the Cubs finish first five times. And then Leo Durocher finished last in 1966.

D.H.

Dear Dr. Die-Hard:

I'm tired of five-year plans. Isn't there some way the Cubs could become instant winners?

Signed,

Impatient

Dear Imp:

Yes. Transfer to the American League West.

D.H.

Dear Dr. Die-Hard:

Some people have told me that Cub fans are un-American because they stay with a loser and accept mediocrity. How do you refute this?

Signed,

John Birch

Dear J.B.:

In the first place, Cub fan's DON'T accept mediocrity. Secondly, when is it un-American to root for the underdog? Since when is hope un-American? Since when is loyalty un-American? Face it, the Cubs are America's Team.

D.H.

Dear Dr. Die-Hard:

My problem is that I never get credit for all I do in my job. I'm not one of the company "stars" but they couldn't get along without me. Any advice?

Signed,

Underdog

Dear Underdog:

Grow as a Cub fan and you will come to understand that unsung heroes may be unsung but they are still heroes. How do you think Harry Steinfelt liked it when Tinker and Evers and Chance were celebrated in poetry and elected to the Hall of Fame? Harry played third base with that trio but you never hear "Steinfelt to Evers to Chance," do you? Still, maybe someday, somebody will remember you just like we're remembering Harry right now.

D.H.

Dear Dr. Die-Hard:

I do my best but it never seems to be quite good enough. How do I avoid disappointment?

Signed,

Discouraged

Dear Discouraged:

You don't have to avoid disappointment. You have to overcome it. Remember Bob Hendley. On September 9, 1965 he pitched a one-hitter against the Dodgers and lost 1-0. Unfortunately, that was the same day Koufax pitched a perfect game against the Cubs. How did Hendley deal with it? Five days later, he pitched a four-hitter and beat Koufax 2-1. Go get 'em!

D.H.

Dear Dr. Die-Hard:

Everything in my life seems to lead nowhere. Everytime I think I'm on my way, I blow it. Help!

Signed,

Flash in the Pan

Dear Flash:

All you need to do is to remember the one and only Roberto Peña. Look up the newspaper accounts of opening day 1965. Roberto was the shortstop. He made three errors. But he also had three hits, one homer, and scored the tying run as the Cubs and Cardinals played to an 11-11 draw. In other words, don't just look at your errors, remember your hits as well.

Or think of Willie Smith. Willie's whole life made him ready for that moment when he was called upon to be great. His two-run pinch homer in the bottom of the 11th started the 1969 Cubs on their winning ways. Your great moment is coming. Be ready.

D.H.

Dear Dr. Die-Hard:

What do you think of the new Cub theme song?

Signed,

Tuned

Dear Tuned:

It's ok, but I'd like to see a composite song representing more of the past and present Cubs. It could open with the theme from "Dallas," then have "He Ain't Heavy, He's My Brother" in honor of Paul Reuschel, "Got Along Without You Before We Met You" for Dave Kingman, and "Stranger in Paradise" for the '69 Cubs. Then it could swing into "It's a Heartache" and end with "If It Takes Forever, I Will Wait For You."

D.H.

8. THE CUB FAN UNMASKED

THE CUB FAN UNMASKED

Better Cub chances
If ways can be found;
Move back the fences,
Lower the mound.

Open the bleachers
To white shirts galore;
Alter the features
Of the foul-line doors.

Fire a white laser
From a scoreboard hole;
Paint the wall azure
And bend the foul pole.

Litter the infield
With pebbles and stones;
Blazon our shield
With skull and bones.

Buy a live bear
To chase foul balls,
To give Mets a scare
And argue close calls.

THE CUB FAN'S GUIDE TO LIFE

Call in a witch
To hex their team,
And make them pitch
What we can cream.

What would it hurt
To use some spit—
Send Mets to the dirt
To avoid being hit.

Offer Muhammed Ali
A starting job;
Teach Mr. T
To slide like Cobb.

Sharpen Cub spikes,
Harden their gaze;
Go for the Bikes
On all close plays.

An exorcist is handy,
An astrologer too;
A hypnotist is dandy,
So is Billy Goat stew.

Get us a flag
We don't care how
Losing's a drag
WE WANT IT NOW!

9. WISDOM TO LIVE BY

WISDOM TO LIVE BY

"The promised land always lies on the other side of a wilderness."
—Havelock Ellis

"It's a good situation here; things can't get any worse. The only way we can go is up."—Larry Bowa in 1981

"They still play a World Series don't they? It's been so long I don't remember."—P.K. Wrigley in 1966

"Baseball is meant for parks like Wrigley Field. It's a personal game. You've got to feel close, get involved. These people would sleep here if they could. So would I."—Ernie Banks

"I would rather be a lamppost in Chicago than a millionaire in any other city."—Cub owner Charles Hulbert in 1876.

"If one system doesn't work, we'll try another. The trouble is that we're already on our third system."
—Owner P.K. Wrigley in 1949

"I'm sick of watching some of my
pitchers getting into jams, then peeping
out to the bullpen to see if a reliever is
ready to take over their work for them. I
want to find out if Cub pitchers have to
have a lantern on home plate to find out
where it's located."—Mgr. Frankie Frisch
in 1950

"The College of Coaches concept is the
best thing that has happened to baseball
since the spitball."—El Tappe in 1961

"It's not where you start, it's where you
finish."—Kermit the Frog

"You have to be prepared for adversity:
it's part of life."—Mgr. Whitey Lockman
after the Cubs blew a three-run lead
in the 9th

"Let your imagination run free. Fantasize
yourself into games. Be the left fielder
who makes a spectacular leaping catch
at the wall to save the game . . . but
sometimes imagine yourself as the hitter
who gave it all he had only to be denied
by that catch."—from THE GAME IS
NEVER OVER

"I don't see how I can fail in
Chicago."—Bump Wills

"If what you did yesterday still looks big to you, you haven't done much today."
—Former Cub general mgr. Wid Matthews

"Harry Chiti is the best kid catcher since Gabby Hartnett."—Wid Matthews

"Unfortunately, pennants aren't won in May."—Mgr. Herman Franks as Cubs move into first on May 30, 1977

"Perfection takes time."—Mgr. Lee Elia after nine-game losing streak in 1982

"You can talk about the loyalty of Dodger fans. They have Tommy Lasorda. That's a good deal, but the Cubs have a better deal. They have me. There is no big Dodger in the sky. God is a Cub fan. As long as there is faith and love in the world, there will be Cub fans."
—Bill Holden

"The worst is not so long as you can say 'This is the worst.' "—William Shakespeare

"Need and struggle are what excite and inspire us."—William James

"Destiny hurts."—Herman Hesse

"The Cubs will be back for more. They have always come back. They always will."
—Sportswriter Warren Brown in 1946

"I have always been an optimist and even though sometimes you lose more than you win with that type of attitude, still and all there are enough great moments, thrills and excitement to make it all beautiful. You know that tommorrow will be a better day."
—Jack Brickhouse

"By just analyzing our team on paper, I say it is possible for us to take all the marbles."—Cub Athletic Director Robert Whitlow in 1962

"So the Cubs haven't won a pennant in nearly forty years. Why not look at it this way? Take it in terms of eternity. That's not even a fly speck. Just tell yourself that sometime in the next thousand years the Cubs will get their share of the pie."—Jack Brickhouse

"Every time I walk onto the field, I can win."—Mgr. Herman Franks in 1977

"The Cubs break your heart one day and have you wondering whether they'll ever win another game. And the next day they look so wonderful they have you floating in the clouds."—Wid Matthews in 1950

"Naturally I'm disappointed the Cubs didn't win. By now, I'm used to disappointments."—P.K. Wrigley in 1969

"Stand tall when the bullets are flying, take the heat, and stay on course." Cub President Jim Finks

"Every player should spend a year with the Cubs to have fun in Wrigley Field." —Al Dark

"If we could have stayed away from the thirteen-game and eight-game losing streaks, there's no telling what we could have accomplished."—Mgr. Lee Elia after the 1982 season

"The 1948 Cubs were the best team ever to finish last in the National League." —General Mgr. Jim Gallagher

"The Cubs didn't fight with each other in my days (the late '50s). We were such a poor hitting club that even if someone did take a swing, he'd miss."
—Jim Brosnan

"This game can be great just as long as you're having fun and don't get caught up in the politics and sour business end of it."—Cub Gary "Sarge" Matthews

"I always was a Cub. When I was playing in Boston and Texas I always used to follow the papers to see how the Cubs were doing. That organization brought me along. I am last of the real Cubs."
—Fergie Jenkins

"When a baseball goes up in the air, it should be caught. When it isn't, it bothers the pitching staff."—Dallas Green

"Baseball is a game with peaks and valleys."—Larry Bowa

"Anyone with a bat in his hands is dangerous."—Bert Wilson

"We also know that this year's rebuilding job has been a flop. But we are not content—and never have been—to just go along with an eye on attendance only.

We want a winner just as you do and we will do everything possible to get one."
—A paid ad placed by the Chicago Cubs in 1948

"If your like your job, it should be fun."
—A sign in the Cub locker room in 1950

"I believe that managers are expendable. In fact, I believe there should be relief managers just like relief pitchers so you can keep rotating them."—P.K. Wrigley in 1959

"Having Hundley catch for you was like sitting down to a steak dinner with a steak knife: without Hundley all you had was a fork."—Fergie Jenkins

10. EXERCISES FOR CUB FANS

EXERCISES FOR CUB FANS

1. Grab a chinning bar (or the top of a door) and pull yourself up until your chin rests on the top. Hang there for as long as you can. When you can't hold on any longer, let yourself fall from exhaustion. Now you know what it must have been like to be a member of the '69 Cubs. That should teach you some empathy and understanding.

2. Take a sharpshooting tennis player to the courts and have him or her stand at one baseline while you position yourself at the center of the opposite baseline. Have the sharpshooter line the ball first to the left corner, then to the right corner, then to the left corner, and so on. Try to race back and forth to cut the ball off. I call this the Frankie Baumholtz maneuver. He did this for six straight months when he played center field between Hank Sauer and Ralph Kiner.

3. On a bright, sunshiny day at 3:00 P.M., take a golfer to a driving range and place yourself 350 feet east of the tee area. You are now facing west. Tell the golfer to hit flies and drives at you. Try to catch them.

I guarantee this exercise will help your speed and footwork as you dodge golf balls. Find yourself ducking? Have trouble following the ball in the sunlight? Now you understand the courage required to play right field at Wrigley.

4. Stay in condition. If you're going to sit half-naked in the bleachers, you need to do your part to beautify America. We want the world to know that Cub fans are beautiful people. When the TV camera combs the bleachers, let's see lean, trim, tan fans. Even more importantly, if you are going to live long enough to see the Cub dynasty win three straight championships, you need to watch your food and drink intake and to exercise daily. As they say in baseball—"you have to be able to look in the mirror."

5. Enter a marathon and sprint for the first 100 yards. Doesn't it feel great to be out in front? Enjoy it. Look back over your shoulder at the mass of opponents pacing themselves. You know that you're almost out of gas and the pack is gaining on you with their relentless, measured sameness. Just as they are about to overtake you, imagine a tape and break it, throwing your arms up in victory. That is your consolation as they pass you by. That is your initiation into understanding Cub history since 1966.

6. Spend a day going to garage sales. Look at all the junk. Select the best of it and bargain for the cheapest price. The stuff you bought may not be as good as the pieces you already have but it may fit in as a nice accent here or there. Now invite your bridge club over and let them see your new pieces. If they sneer or laugh, if they tell you you were robbed, if they tell you that your furnishings look worse instead of better, you will know how Bob Kennedy felt when he met the press to announce an acquisition or a trade.

11. HOW TO DEAL WITH SUCCESS

HOW TO DEAL WITH SUCCESS

When the Cubs beat their Iowa AAA farm team in 1984, it seemed to be just one more sign, one more confirmation that this is a team of destiny. It was the first time in four years that the Chicago Cubs defeated the Iowa Cubs and it helped erase the embarrassment of hearing the Iowa fans chant in 1981, "Don't send anyone down, don't send anyone down."

As writers and wags and humorists began to take the 1984 Cubs seriously a whole spate of articles appeared wondering what Cub fans would do if their favorites actually won the pennant. Some suggested that, having achieved the goal, Cub fans would find that the fun was gone, that if they were no longer the underdog the quest would lose its mystique. Others thought that Cub fans would be driven to find a new door-mat they could cheer for. Like the Seattle Mariners. Still others predicted that Cub fans would literally go crazy in a frenzy of fulfillment that would tear down the North Side of Chicago.

To all of these theories, I say, "Malarky!"
No one understands better than a Cub fan
the fleeting nature of glory. We'll take it
when it comes. We'll be grateful for it. We'll
be thrilled to win our division—ecstatic to
win the League Championship—and in a
state of nirvana to win the World Series.

But winning will not spoil us.

We have not nor will we ever make winning the pennant a condition for our allegiance. We are not like Yankee fans.

Since we don't love the Cubs *because*
they lose, we will not be motivated to aban-
don them when they win. Unlike Mets fans,
we can cheer a loser without being losers.

And we will not tear down the North
Side. We are not by nature raucous. Like
you know who.

Cub fans will take winning in stride. With
enthusiam, with tears of joy, perhaps, but
in stride.

When it happens you will find us, like
our ancestors in 1908, sensitive enough to
know how to be humble in the face of a
miracle.

THE DIAMOND COLLECTION . . .

CALENDARS
The Cub Fan's Calendar 1985 . . . . $7.95
The Detroit Tiger Fan's Calendar 1985 . $9.95
The Padre Fan's Calendar 1985 . . . . $7.95

BOOKS
The Cub Fan's Guide to Life $3.95
Grimm's Baseball Tales $7.95
The Game is Never Over: An Appreciative
   History of the Chicago Cubs $7.95
I ♥ the Cubs Coloring Book $2.00
The Cub Fan's Christmas Wish $3.50

POSTERS
The Love of Baseball $4.95
Waiting for a Pennant $4.95

COLLECTOR'S SPECIAL
The Cub Fan's Calendar 1983
The Cub Fan's Calendar 1984
       $10 ea. or both for $15.00

Send your orders plus $1.50 for shipping to:

DIAMOND COMMUNICATIONS, INC.
P.O. BOX 94
NOTRE DAME, IN 46556

Or Call:

(219) 287-5008
VISA/MASTERCARD ACCEPTED